I BELIEVE

One man's views on

marriage, children,

the state of the union,

existentialism, the

best movies ever, the

perfect gin and tonic,

blueberries, the

historic significance of

remote controls,

tattoos, heaven and

hell, etc.

I BELIEVE

Tom,
What do you believe?
Allan Stark
2-3-00

Allan Stark

STARK
BOOKS
an Andrews McMeel
Publishing Imprint

00 01 02 03 04 RDC 10 9 8 7 6 5 4 3 2 1

Library of Congress Cataloging-in-Publication Data

Stark, Allan, 1951-
  I believe / Allan Stark.
    p. cm.
  ISBN 0-7407-0570-9 (pbk.)
  1. Life-Miscellanea. 2. Stark, Allan, 1951—Miscellanea. I. Title.
  BD435.S743 2000
  081-dc21   99-57366

Book design by Holly Camerlinck

Attention: Schools and Businesses

Andrews McMeel books are available at quantity discounts with bulk purchase for educational, business, or sales promotional use. For information, please write to: Special Sales Department, Andrews McMeel Publishing, 4520 Main Street, Kansas City, Missouri 64111.

To my mother, Barbara, whom I miss
To my father, Gordon, whom I still depend upon
To my wife, Nancy, whom I love
To my children, Cate and Ruth, whom I cherish

INTRODUCTION

◆ ◆ ◆

I was born at the University of Kansas Medical Center on December 24, 1951. I am a white male with a wife, two daughters, a used minivan, and a 1992 Volvo four-door sedan. We had a yellow Lab named Søren. He was the best dog in the world. We had to put him to sleep on January 5, 2000, just two days after his thirteenth birthday.

I went to a public elementary school in Kansas City, Missouri (Bryant), a private boys' school for junior high and high school (Pembroke–Country Day), and to Trinity College in Hartford, Connecticut. I majored in religion, which I am still trying to explain to my family and friends. I have been a teacher, a coach, a sportswriter, an editor, and a salesman. I am very lucky to have a wife who is patient and has a sense of humor. My father is alive. My mother died in 1997. I usually get to work early. Golf is my addiction of choice. I go to church reasonably frequently.

That is what I am. And what I am is neither good nor bad. The facts—the past—can't be changed, and facts alone don't ever tell the whole story about a person. They can tell you what I am and what I do, but they don't tell you who I am or what I think.

What motivated me to start examining and writing down my beliefs? It was the 1988 baseball movie *Bull Durham,* which starred Kevin Costner, Susan Sarandon, and Tim Robbins. I thought the movie was wonderful, but there is one scene that left an indelible impression on me.

Here's the setup for the scene: The veteran minor-league catcher Crash Davis (Costner) and the rookie pitching sensation Nuke (Robbins) are invited to visit Annie Savoy (Susan Sarandon). Annie is a baseball groupie who chooses a Durham Bulls player each season to love. The two players are informed that one of them will be the lucky player, and, in effect, they are there to audition for the job.

Crash, a twelve-year veteran who was signed by the Bulls to be Nuke's mentor, doesn't believe he should have to audition for Annie's heart. In fact, Crash decides to leave and informs Annie that she would be far better off if she would consider only men who could think and articulate their opinions.

Annie then asks Crash about his opinions—his beliefs. He answers with this:

Well, I believe in the soul . . . the small of a woman's back, the hangin' curveball, high fiber, good Scotch, that the novels of Susan Sontag are self-indulgent, overrated crap. I believe Lee Harvey Oswald acted alone, I believe there ought to be a constitutional amendment outlawing AstroTurf . . . I believe in the sweet spot, soft-core pornography, opening your presents Christmas morning rather than Christmas Eve, and I believe in long, slow, deep, wet kisses that last three days.

It wasn't *what* Crash believed that caught my attention; it was that he *knew* what he believed. He had thought about his beliefs and had taken the time to memorize them. I knew I had beliefs, but I also realized they were nothing more than a random collection of thoughts.

I Believe is not intended to be a reference book for those looking for beliefs. Rather, think of this as an inspirational book. The sole intention of *I Believe* is to make you think about your beliefs and about why having beliefs is important.

Beliefs, above all else, are personal and, as a result, define the individual. Beliefs can be serious, funny, interesting, trivial, judgmental, objective, off-the-wall, or well-researched.

The idea is to think. Think about you, your family, your friends, your experiences, your job, your hobbies, your passions, and your dreams, and then think about what you as an individual truly believe.

1.

I believe the mind and body can work together to fight disease, but thank God there are lots of good doctors.

◆ ◆ ◆

2.

I believe Helen Keller was one of the most courageous Americans in our history.

◆ ◆ ◆

3.

I believe Jesus Christ died too young, but it must have been God's will.

◆ ◆ ◆

4.

I believe professional athletes should accept the fact that they **are** *role models.*

◆ ◆ ◆

5.

I believe in saying "good morning" to my neighbors.

◆ ◆ ◆

6.

I believe companies should make commitments to cities instead of looking for tax breaks.

◆ ◆ ◆

7.

I believe Jackie Robinson helped make America a better place.

◆ ◆ ◆

8.

I believe Michael Jordan had one more **great** *year in him.*

◆ ◆ ◆

9.

I believe my mother is in heaven **and** *that she* **will** *always let me know what she thinks of my decisions.*

◆ ◆ ◆

10.

I believe my grandmother is in heaven **and**
that she will always love me
unconditionally.

◆ ◆ ◆

11.

I believe everyone should see W. C. Fields in
the movie **It's a Gift.**

◆ ◆ ◆

12.

I believe Mike Tyson could have been the
second greatest fighter ever—if not for his
behavioral problems.

◆ ◆ ◆

13.

I believe there are two kinds of lawyers in the world—constructive and destructive.

❖ ❖ ❖

14.

I believe blueberries are the best berries.

❖ ❖ ❖

15.

I believe Tattered Cover in Denver is North America's best independent bookstore.

❖ ❖ ❖

16.

I believe John Irving's **The World According to Garp** *is the most entertaining American novel written in the last forty years.*

◆ ◆ ◆

17.

I believe you should turn off your cell phone in church, in restaurants, at lunch, at the movies, on the golf course, and at school plays and concerts.

◆ ◆ ◆

18.

I believe William Wegman's dog photos are "too too."

◆ ◆ ◆

19.

*I believe in always keeping the wind at
your back when playing golf
and sailing.*

◆ ◆ ◆

20.

*I believe the SUV craze is getting
way out of hand.*

◆ ◆ ◆

21.

*I believe in ZPG
(zero population growth).*

◆ ◆ ◆

22.

I believe Joe Montana was a better quarterback than John Elway— but not by much.

◆ ◆ ◆

23.

I believe that technology is not user-friendly. (Of course, I have to admit that I am not very friendly to technology.)

◆ ◆ ◆

24.

*I believe Mike Royko was the best
big-city columnist ever. (By the way,
the big city is Chicago, and he wrote for
the* Daily News, *the* Sun-Times, *and
the* Tribune.)

◆ ◆ ◆

25.

I believe The Phantom Menace *was
good but not great.*

◆ ◆ ◆

26.

*I believe Columbine High School
should change its name to
Dave Sanders High School.
(Sanders was the teacher who was killed
trying to save the lives of his students.)*

◆ ◆ ◆

27.

*I believe in saying "please" and
"thank you."*

◆ ◆ ◆

28.

*I believe Michael Jackson not so secretly
wants to be Diana Ross.*

◆ ◆ ◆

29.

I believe letter writing

is a lost art.

30.

I believe there are differences between men and women—not that there's anything wrong with that.

◆ ◆ ◆

31.

I believe you should be loyal to your home team even if it loses more often than it wins.

◆ ◆ ◆

32.

I believe in buying a car you can afford instead of the car you want.

◆ ◆ ◆

33.

*I believe Target is the best
mass-market merchandiser.*

◆ ◆ ◆

34.

I believe children are a godsend.

◆ ◆ ◆

35.

*I believe mothers-in-law are either good
news or bad news. (Just for the record, my
mother-in-law, Mimi, is great.)*

◆ ◆ ◆

36.

I believe in wearing sunscreen.

◆ ◆ ◆

37.

*I believe Midwest Express is the best
airline in North America.*

◆ ◆ ◆

38.

*I believe George Steinbrenner is missing
the loyalty gene.*

◆ ◆ ◆

39.

I believe modesty is a virtue.

◆ ◆ ◆

40.

*I believe parents must accept the fact that
they are role models for their children.*

◆ ◆ ◆

41.

I believe in using rechargeable batteries.

◆ ◆ ◆

42.

I believe **The Lion King** *is the best Disney animated movie ever.*

◆ ◆ ◆

43.

I believe that casinos and the Psychic Network have much in common.

◆ ◆ ◆

44.

I believe hell on Earth is the middle seat on a crowded airplane.

◆ ◆ ◆

45.

I believe in knowing your competition.

◆ ◆ ◆

46.

I believe our politicians will continue to disappoint us until they change the campaign financing laws.

◆ ◆ ◆

47.

I believe in the American dream.

◆ ◆ ◆

48.

I believe Tim Russert is the best political analyst on TV.

◆ ◆ ◆

49.

I believe too many lawsuits are nothing more than legalized blackmail scams.

◆ ◆ ◆

50.

I believe Pavarotti should lose seventy-five pounds and go back to his first wife.

◆ ◆ ◆

51.

I believe Mick Jagger should accept the fact that he is over fifty.

◆ ◆ ◆

52.

I believe trust is the basis
of all friendships.

53.

*I believe in supporting local stores
instead of faraway catalog companies—
whenever possible.*

◆ ◆ ◆

54.

*I believe that Nelson Mandela is a man
of courage and conviction.*

◆ ◆ ◆

55.

*I believe Catholic priests should be
allowed to marry.*

◆ ◆ ◆

56.

I believe Shaquille O'Neal should work as hard at becoming a 75 percent free throw shooter as he does at becoming a movie star.

◆ ◆ ◆

57.

I believe parents should get to know their children's teachers.

◆ ◆ ◆

58.

I believe Dave Barry is the funniest writer in America.

◆ ◆ ◆

59.

I believe cats like being aloof.

◆ ◆ ◆

60.

*I believe teachers, firemen, and policemen
are underpaid!*

◆ ◆ ◆

61.

*I believe the morning paper should be
delivered by 5:00 A.M.*

◆ ◆ ◆

62.

*I believe in doing what my boss tells
me to do.*

◆ ◆ ◆

63.

I believe Gennifer Flowers told the truth.

◆ ◆ ◆

64.

I believe Paula Jones told the truth.

◆ ◆ ◆

65.

I believe Kathleen Willey told the truth.

◆ ◆ ◆

66.

*I believe Monica Lewinsky didn't
tell the whole truth.*

◆ ◆ ◆

67.

I believe in setting goals.

◆ ◆ ◆

68.

*I believe in making realistic
New Year's resolutions.*

◆ ◆ ◆

69.

*I believe in carrying plenty of
business cards.*

◆ ◆ ◆

70.

*I believe in carrying a picture of my wife
and children in my wallet.*

◆ ◆ ◆

71.

I believe in firm handshakes.

◆ ◆ ◆

72.

I believe in eye contact when you are talking to someone.

◆ ◆ ◆

73.

I believe in term limits for all elected officials.

◆ ◆ ◆

74.

I believe Kansas City barbecue is the best barbecue.

◆ ◆ ◆

75.

*I believe mankind must do everything
in its power to save the tiger.*

◆ ◆ ◆

76.

*I believe that you can believe in the
Bible and in evolution.*

◆ ◆ ◆

77.

*I believe in staying within five miles per
hour of the speed limit in the city and eight
miles per hour on the highway.*

◆ ◆ ◆

78.

*I believe Ralph Nader has helped
to make the world a better place.*

◆ ◆ ◆

79.

*I believe in being on time for appointments
and ten minutes late to parties.*

◆ ◆ ◆

80.

*I believe the best salesmen are closing
on Friday afternoons.*

◆ ◆ ◆

81.

I believe in the New World Order.

◆ ◆ ◆

82.

I believe Jake and Elwood **were** *on a mission from God.*

◆ ◆ ◆

83.

I believe I could survive on peanut M&M's.

◆ ◆ ◆

84.

I believe in keeping score.

◆ ◆ ◆

85.

I believe revenge can be a very good motivator.

◆ ◆ ◆

86.

I believe in diving for the loose ball.

◆ ◆ ◆

87.

I believe "joy" is one of the most descriptive words in the English language.

◆ ◆ ◆

88.

I believe Dennis Miller is a tragically hip, overly judgmental, smarter-than-all-of-the-rest-of-us, angst-ridden, wish-he-had-actually-done-something-interesting-in-his-life, wanna-be-ultrafamous entertainer.

◆ ◆ ◆

89.

*I believe being happy is a
good choice, not a "courageous" one,
as Sharon Stone says.*

◆ ◆ ◆

90.

*I believe I need to be more patient
with my children.*

◆ ◆ ◆

91.

*I believe race car drivers have more guts
than common sense.*

◆ ◆ ◆

92.

*I believe steaks taste best when
cooked outside over a charcoal fire
with hickory chips.*

◆ ◆ ◆

93.

I believe in wearing natural fibers.

◆ ◆ ◆

94.

*I believe it's possible to keep a marriage fun,
surprising, and spontaneous
(even if you have children).*

◆ ◆ ◆

95.

I believe everyone has potential.

◆ ◆ ◆

96.

I believe everyone can improve.

◆ ◆ ◆

97.

*I believe good cookware does
make life easier.*

◆ ◆ ◆

98.

I believe tall people are
damn lucky.

99.

I believe skinny people are either lucky or very disciplined.

◆ ◆ ◆

100.

I believe it's important to tell your spouse how much you love her or him.

◆ ◆ ◆

101.

I believe I would feel out of place at a nude beach. (Actually, I know I would.)

◆ ◆ ◆

102.

*I believe a bagel is only a bagel
if it is boiled.*

◆ ◆ ◆

103.

*I believe hell is a place where everyone
is beautiful and rich, has a tan,
knows it all, laughs at every joke,
sinks every putt, drives a nice car,
never gains an ounce . . .*

◆ ◆ ◆

104.

*I believe you need to put at least a little
butter on popcorn.*

◆ ◆ ◆

105.

I believe in keeping my car clean.

◆ ◆ ◆

106.

I believe a yellow light means:
"Stop if you can."

◆ ◆ ◆

107.

I believe in saving money for my
retirement and for my children.

◆ ◆ ◆

108.

I believe life goes by way too fast.

◆ ◆ ◆

109.

*I believe in stopping my car and
helping turtles across the road.*

◆ ◆ ◆

110.

*I believe you need to take
your sense of humor to work every day.*

◆ ◆ ◆

111.

I believe attitude is everything.

◆ ◆ ◆

112.

*I believe the follow-up is the key
to selling.*

◆ ◆ ◆

113.

I believe schools should concentrate on the basics: reading, writing, and arithmetic.

❖ ❖ ❖

114.

I believe Marilyn Monroe was misunderstood but was **impossible** *to understand.*

❖ ❖ ❖

115.

I believe Søren Kierkegaard is the father of existentialism.

❖ ❖ ❖

116.

I believe **The Stranger** *was Albert Camus's best book.*

◆ ◆ ◆

117.

I believe in compound interest.

◆ ◆ ◆

118.

I believe regular exercise relieves stress.

◆ ◆ ◆

119.

I believe that you are never too old to learn something new.

◆ ◆ ◆

120.

*I believe in hiring people who are
smarter than I am.*

◆ ◆ ◆

121.

*I believe it when my children tell me,
"I love you."*

◆ ◆ ◆

122.

*I believe Bryant Gumbel has very good
taste in clothes.*

◆ ◆ ◆

123.

I believe Woody Allen needs to spend at least two hours a day in therapy.

◆ ◆ ◆

124.

I believe in trying to look your best.

◆ ◆ ◆

125.

I believe Ann Coulter is the only Republican who could beat Bill Clinton in a debate.

◆ ◆ ◆

126.

I believe that our founding fathers would ban handguns if they were alive today.

◆ ◆ ◆

127.

I believe Bob Packwood and Bill Clinton are two peas in a pod.

◆ ◆ ◆

128.

I believe "hugs" is a wonderfully warm and active word.

◆ ◆ ◆

129.

I believe Chicago will always be our second city. (L.A. just doesn't have a heart.)

◆ ◆ ◆

130.

I believe you need the following for the perfect winter night at home: a real fire, flannel PJs, a bottle of wine, a great movie or video, and a hand to hold.

◆ ◆ ◆

131.

I believe Anthony Robbins can make me happier, healthier, richer, and more fit for $179.85 (postage not included).

◆ ◆ ◆

132.

I believe language tapes are pretty useless for anyone over twenty-one.

◆ ◆ ◆

133.

I believe radical wraparound sunglasses should be worn by young people **only**.

◆ ◆ ◆

134.

I believe only real cowboys should wear cowboy hats. (A Halloween party is the only exception to that rule.)

◆ ◆ ◆

135.

I believe the world is an oyster
that can be cracked with a little effort.

◆ ◆ ◆

136.

I believe the 1980 U.S. Olympic hockey
team defines the word "miraculous."

◆ ◆ ◆

137.

I believe in watching the weather
forecast before I leave town.

◆ ◆ ◆

138.

I believe Crested Butte with its mining town charm is North America's friendliest ski resort.

◆ ◆ ◆

139.

I believe everyone should visit the Grand Canyon.

◆ ◆ ◆

140.

I believe in listening to **unabridged** *book tapes.*

◆ ◆ ◆

141.

I believe in plastic surgery
if it makes you feel better
about yourself.

142.

*I believe I should use coupons;
unfortunately, I don't always do
what I should.*

◆ ◆ ◆

143.

I believe in gut instinct.

◆ ◆ ◆

144.

I believe in sharing what I know.

◆ ◆ ◆

145.

I believe in admitting my mistakes.

◆ ◆ ◆

146.

I believe John McEnroe was a great tennis player **and** *an unbelievable brat.*

◆ ◆ ◆

147.

I believe in going beyond one's comfort zone.

◆ ◆ ◆

148.

I believe heroes are normal people who know their limitations but choose to challenge them.

◆ ◆ ◆

149.

I believe companies that welcome ideas with open arms understand that growth is essential.

◆ ◆ ◆

150.

I believe creative people know how to balance reality and fantasy.

◆ ◆ ◆

151.

I believe in reaching for the stars.

◆ ◆ ◆

152.

I believe all successful people have made more than their fair share of mistakes.

◆ ◆ ◆

153.

I believe in kissing my wife and children in the morning and as soon as I get home.

◆ ◆ ◆

154.

I believe courage is contagious.

◆ ◆ ◆

155.

I believe in being decisive.

◆ ◆ ◆

156.

*I believe everyone has at least one talent
that he or she takes for granted.*

◆ ◆ ◆

157.

I believe in the Prime Directive.

◆ ◆ ◆

158.

I believe O.J. killed Nicole and Ron.

◆ ◆ ◆

159.

*I believe Yoko Ono is responsible for
the breakup of the Beatles.*

◆ ◆ ◆

160.

*I believe Bob Dylan brought in
the 1960s.*

◆ ◆ ◆

161.

*I believe religion is a matter
of faith, not logic!*

◆ ◆ ◆

162.

I believe Prince Charles is a cold fish.

◆ ◆ ◆

163.

I believe Jimmy Swaggart knows more ladies of the evening than Bible verses.

◆ ◆ ◆

164.

I believe baseball should be played on grass.

◆ ◆ ◆

165.

I believe in love at first sight.

◆ ◆ ◆

166.

I believe Princess Di is in heaven.

◆ ◆ ◆

167.

I believe in Santa Claus.

◆ ◆ ◆

168.

*I believe kissing and making up
is one of the best things
about marriage.*

◆ ◆ ◆

169.

I believe nature is at its best during fall.

◆ ◆ ◆

170.

I believe wisdom comes with age.

◆ ◆ ◆

171.

*I believe I would enjoy talking to **any** of the people in **any** of Edward Hopper's paintings.*

◆ ◆ ◆

172.

*I believe the eyes are
the windows into the soul.*

◆ ◆ ◆

173.

*I believe Dr. Pepper is America's
best soft drink.*

◆ ◆ ◆

174.

I believe in hard work.

◆ ◆ ◆

175.

I believe Marv Albert should have gone to jail.

◆ ◆ ◆

176.

I believe the dog is man's best friend.

◆ ◆ ◆

177.

I believe Monopoly is the most entertaining board game ever invented. (I believe in buying houses and hotels as soon as I can.)

◆ ◆ ◆

178.

I believe Coke is better than Pepsi.

◆ ◆ ◆

179.

I believe great service builds loyalty.

◆ ◆ ◆

180.

*I believe McDonald's has the best
fast-food coffee.*

◆ ◆ ◆

181.

I believe in God.

◆ ◆ ◆

182.

*I believe Los Angeles will eventually
grind to a halt.*

◆ ◆ ◆

183.

I believe Mardi Gras is the
greatest party on Earth.

184.

I believe the NHL and NBA seasons are too long. Neither sport should be played in June.

◆ ◆ ◆

185.

I believe Martha Stewart is perfect—
at least on TV.

◆ ◆ ◆

186.

I believe TV is good **and** *bad.*

◆ ◆ ◆

187.

I believe a smile can turn a person's
day around.

◆ ◆ ◆

188.

*I believe Absolut is the best vodka
in the world.*

◆ ◆ ◆

189.

*I believe Bob Costas would be a great
commissioner of baseball.*

◆ ◆ ◆

190.

*I believe in becoming acquainted
with one's limitations.*

◆ ◆ ◆

191.

*I believe Wal-Mart needs to
landscape its parking lots.*

◆ ◆ ◆

192.

*I believe Baltimore's Camden Yards is
baseball's heaven on earth.*

◆ ◆ ◆

193.

*I believe women—and women only—
should decide the abortion issue.*

◆ ◆ ◆

194.

I believe Dilbert needs a girlfriend.

◆ ◆ ◆

195.

*I believe every American should visit
the Washington Monument, the Lincoln
Memorial, and the Vietnam
Veterans Memorial.*

◆ ◆ ◆

196.

*I believe Cal Ripken's consecutive game
playing record will stand forever.*

◆ ◆ ◆

197.

*I believe a restaurant will succeed
if the hot food is hot, the cold drinks
are cold, and the waiters are friendly.*

◆ ◆ ◆

198.

I believe in taking my children to the park for long walks.

◆ ◆ ◆

199.

I believe whiners are bores.

◆ ◆ ◆

200.

I believe the vows of marriage should be taken seriously.

◆ ◆ ◆

201.

I believe the customer is **usually** *right.*

◆ ◆ ◆

202.

*I believe that middle-aged men should
think twice before taking a fashion risk.*

◆ ◆ ◆

203.

*I believe it's better to be overdressed
than underdressed.*

◆ ◆ ◆

204.

*I believe that excuses are
just that—excuses.*

◆ ◆ ◆

205.

I believe my dog has a soul.

◆ ◆ ◆

206.

I believe every thirteen-year-old should read **The Catcher in the Rye.**

◆ ◆ ◆

207.

I believe Gary Larson and Bill Watterson should come out of retirement and start drawing **The Far Side** *and* **Calvin and Hobbes** *again.*

◆ ◆ ◆

208.

I believe Al Gore should become director of the Boy Scouts of America.

◆ ◆ ◆

209.

I believe you should leave your children at home when you go to Las Vegas.

❖ ❖ ❖

210.

I believe practice makes perfect (or at least will help).

❖ ❖ ❖

211.

I believe in "buckling up."

❖ ❖ ❖

212.

I believe Lee Harvey Oswald was just a patsy.

❖ ❖ ❖

213.

*I believe it always pays to be polite
to police officers.*

◆ ◆ ◆

214.

I believe in the five basic food groups.

◆ ◆ ◆

215.

*I believe infomercials were invented
to exploit the weaknesses of insomniacs.*

◆ ◆ ◆

216.

*I believe certain occasions call for a big
steak and a great bottle of red wine.*

◆ ◆ ◆

217.

I believe Lee jeans fit the average person better than Levi's.

◆ ◆ ◆

218.

I believe cigars are only cigars.

◆ ◆ ◆

219.

I believe in doing your homework.

◆ ◆ ◆

220.

I believe in writing the president of the company when you have a complaint or a compliment.

◆ ◆ ◆

221.

I believe the United States needs to support Israel financially.

◆ ◆ ◆

222.

I believe Scientology is more business than religion.

◆ ◆ ◆

223.

I believe in speaking to your audience, not over it.

◆ ◆ ◆

224.

I believe Jackie O. put her children first.

◆ ◆ ◆

225.

I believe Jimmy Carter has a kind heart.

◆ ◆ ◆

226.

I believe in thank-you notes.

◆ ◆ ◆

227.

I believe in the First Amendment,
but I believe we must use some
common sense when interpreting it.

◆ ◆ ◆

228.

I believe cabdrivers should be able
to speak English.

◆ ◆ ◆

229.

I believe in asking for directions when I'm lost—unless, of course, I am pretty sure I know where I am going.

◆ ◆ ◆

230.

I believe in keeping a secret.

◆ ◆ ◆

231.

I believe in the Ten Commandments.

◆ ◆ ◆

232.

I believe you are born either straight or gay.

◆ ◆ ◆

233.

I believe in acts of kindness.

◆ ◆ ◆

234.

I believe that you should learn something new every day.

◆ ◆ ◆

235.

I believe swing sets are enjoyed equally by children and adults.

◆ ◆ ◆

236.

I believe in using the turn signal for lane changes.

◆ ◆ ◆

237.

*I believe every day is a bad hair day
for Donald Trump.*

◆ ◆ ◆

238.

I believe **Law & Order** *is the
best drama on TV.*

◆ ◆ ◆

239.

*I believe America is the
greatest country on Earth.*

◆ ◆ ◆

240.

I believe Canada is the second best.

◆ ◆ ◆

241.

I believe a martini should be very dry.

◆ ◆ ◆

242.

*I believe the innocence of youth should be
protected for as long as possible.*

◆ ◆ ◆

243.

*I believe in being the first one to apologize
even if I wasn't the one in the wrong.*

◆ ◆ ◆

244.

*I believe children need lots of hugs
and kisses.*

◆ ◆ ◆

245.

I believe America's ethnic
differences will eventually
become one of its strengths.

246.

I believe in Martin Luther King's dream.

◆ ◆ ◆

247.

*I believe Bill Clinton will go down
in history as a great politician and
a lousy president.*

◆ ◆ ◆

248.

*I believe most incumbents care more
about being reelected than about
voting their conscience.*

◆ ◆ ◆

249.

I believe the movie **Gone With The Wind** *is way too long.*

◆ ◆ ◆

250.

I believe there's a good chance I won't survive the adolescent years of my daughters.

◆ ◆ ◆

251.

I believe blondes are just as smart as the rest of us.

◆ ◆ ◆

252.

I believe I could handle the problems
associated with wealth.

◆ ◆ ◆

253.

I believe **Seinfeld's** George should get
a full-time job before it's too late.

◆ ◆ ◆

254.

I believe David Letterman should be
nicer to his guests.

◆ ◆ ◆

255.

I believe time flies.

◆ ◆ ◆

256.

*I believe French philosopher and
mathematician René Descartes was
right when he said, "It is not enough
to have a good mind. The main thing
is to use it well."*

❖ ❖ ❖

257.

I believe some people are just born happy.

❖ ❖ ❖

258.

I believe Elvis is dead.

❖ ❖ ❖

259.

I believe the Warren Report is fiction.

◆ ◆ ◆

260.

*I believe politicians throughout the world
need to think about the next two or three
generations, not just the next two or
three years.*

◆ ◆ ◆

261.

*I believe in the separation of church
and state.*

◆ ◆ ◆

262.

I believe life is what
you make it.

263.

I believe bosses need to set good examples.

◆ ◆ ◆

264.

I believe it's important to be enthusiastic at work and play.

◆ ◆ ◆

265.

I believe all families are crazy and that's why all families are interesting.

◆ ◆ ◆

266.

*I believe tank tops are a **big** fashion mistake for men!*

◆ ◆ ◆

267.

I believe Bill Russell is the greatest team player in the history of the NBA.

◆ ◆ ◆

268.

I believe Barbra Streisand is a wonderful entertainer who takes the rest of life too seriously. (And I believe James Brolin has a great thing going with Barbra.)

◆ ◆ ◆

269.

*I believe Yugoslav president
Slobodan Milosevic is a mass murderer.*

◆ ◆ ◆

270.

*I believe we should pray for the souls
of Eric Harris and Dylan Klebold—
but it is not easy to do.*

◆ ◆ ◆

271.

*I believe we must figure out a way to
protect our children from offensive
content on TV and the Internet.*

◆ ◆ ◆

272.

I believe Jesse Jackson is well-intentioned.

◆ ◆ ◆

273.

*I believe parenthood is a
serious obligation.*

◆ ◆ ◆

274.

*I believe I could look at Vincent van Gogh's
painting* **The Starry Night** *all day.*

◆ ◆ ◆

275.

*I believe citizens have an obligation
to take part in the democratic process.
In other words, vote!*

◆ ◆ ◆

276.

I believe The Force is within all of us.

◆ ◆ ◆

277.

*I believe Siegfried & Roy have the best
show in Las Vegas (but you have to admit,
they* **are** *a bit unusual).*

◆ ◆ ◆

278.

I believe **Death of a Salesman** *is*
the *American play.*

◆ ◆ ◆

279.

I believe teams win championships
for two reasons: better players and
better coaches.

◆ ◆ ◆

280.

I believe it's okay to talk about religion
and politics with your friends.

◆ ◆ ◆

281.

I believe conversation is
becoming a lost art.

282.

*I believe children need to have rules
and limitations.*

◆ ◆ ◆

283.

*I believe in taking lots of photographs and
videos of my family and friends.*

◆ ◆ ◆

284.

*I believe the ability to get along with people
is a real talent that shouldn't be
taken for granted.*

◆ ◆ ◆

285.

I believe I exist.

◆ ◆ ◆

286.

I believe Hitler was pure evil.

◆ ◆ ◆

287.

*I believe God's greatest gift to mankind
is free will.*

◆ ◆ ◆

288.

*I believe in making a big deal
out of birthdays—even for those of us
who are over forty.*

◆ ◆ ◆

289.

I believe life is enhanced by regularly having family and friends over for casual, conversation-filled dinners.

◆ ◆ ◆

290.

I believe Jay Leno is the best right now, but Johnny Carson is still the king of late-night TV.

◆ ◆ ◆

291.

I believe beavers are nature's master builders.

◆ ◆ ◆

292.

*I believe teenagers will be
listening to—and enjoying—Jimi Hendrix
for the next fifty years.*

◆ ◆ ◆

293.

I believe in giving to charity.

◆ ◆ ◆

294.

*I believe in subscribing to my
local newspaper.*

◆ ◆ ◆

295.

*I believe space exploration is essential
if mankind is going to survive another
thousand years on Earth.*

◆ ◆ ◆

296.

*I believe the least government
is the best government.*

◆ ◆ ◆

297.

*I believe caller ID is preserving
my sanity.*

◆ ◆ ◆

298.

I believe E.T.—The Extra-Terrestrial
*should have been ranked in the top ten
by the American Film Institute in its poll
of the One Hundred Best American
Movies of all time.*

◆ ◆ ◆

299.
*I believe only a handful of people
really enjoy going to the opera.
Everybody else is there to be seen.*

◆ ◆ ◆

300.

*I believe unions could have a bright future
if they were willing to tie their raises
and benefits to corporate profits.*

◆ ◆ ◆

301.

*I believe losing those five extra pounds
gets harder with every passing year.*

◆ ◆ ◆

302.

*I believe two Rocky movies
would have been enough.*

◆ ◆ ◆

303.

I believe next year will be my best year.
(I say that every New Year's Eve.)

◆ ◆ ◆

304.

I believe Hillary Clinton should have
thrown the bum out of the house.

◆ ◆ ◆

305.

I believe you can be too thin, but I am
not so sure about too rich.

◆ ◆ ◆

306.

I believe the government should look for ways to save money instead of ways to spend more.

◆ ◆ ◆

307.

I believe Russia will eventually become a fully working democracy.

◆ ◆ ◆

308.

I believe my grandmother's generation (she was born in 1899 and died in 1986) experienced more dramatic social, technological, and economic changes than any generation in history.

◆ ◆ ◆

309.

I believe the drug war is a war we must fight to win even if that means using the military.

◆ ◆ ◆

310.

I believe I could spend a week at the San Diego Zoo and Wild Animal Park.

◆ ◆ ◆

311.

I believe the governments of the world should set aside their differences and make a real effort to save as many endangered animals as possible.

◆ ◆ ◆

312.

I believe the Rolling Stones are the greatest rock 'n' roll band of all time.

◆ ◆ ◆

313.

I believe the **New York Times** *needs to improve its sports section.*

◆ ◆ ◆

314.

I believe **The Princess Bride** *is the funniest and wittiest family movie ever.*

◆ ◆ ◆

315.

I believe I should read more.

◆ ◆ ◆

316.

I believe older people deserve my respect.

◆ ◆ ◆

317.

I believe all of my decades (starting with the 1950s) have been interesting.

◆ ◆ ◆

318.

I believe jealousy is a real waste of time.

◆ ◆ ◆

319.

I believe in thinking long term when it comes to saving for my children's college educations.

◆ ◆ ◆

320.

I believe that I will eventually find the perfect job.

◆ ◆ ◆

321.

I believe everyone is entitled to his or her own opinion. (Of course, it would be nice if their opinions were based on some knowledge.)

◆ ◆ ◆

322.

I believe in keeping receipts and/or guarantees for all of my major purchases.

◆ ◆ ◆

323.

I believe **GoodFellas** *is the ultimate "guy" movie.*

◆ ◆ ◆

324.

I believe Katie Couric is smart **and** *perky.*

◆ ◆ ◆

325.

*I believe the Outward Bound schools
teach teamwork* **and** *self-reliance.*

◆ ◆ ◆

326.

*I believe I have the nicest and sweetest
wife in the world.*

◆ ◆ ◆

327.

*I believe people should stand behind
their work.*

◆ ◆ ◆

328.

I believe some of the most interesting conversations happen *after* one more drink.

329.

I believe Labs are the friendliest dogs.

◆ ◆ ◆

330.

I believe Chris Van Allsburg's
The Polar Express *is the best-written
and best-illustrated children's book
ever published.*

◆ ◆ ◆

331.

*I believe Rush Limbaugh is bombastic,
outrageous, and very entertaining.*

◆ ◆ ◆

332.

I believe Dan Gable's 1972 Olympic
wrestling victory in the 149-pound weight
class is the greatest individual performance
in Olympic history. He literally dominated
the competition.

◆ ◆ ◆

333.

I believe a salesman will be successful if
he knows his product, shows up for
appointments on time, and follows up.

◆ ◆ ◆

334.

I believe in hanging mistletoe in the
front hall during the holidays.

◆ ◆ ◆

335.

*I believe every dessert should
include chocolate.*

◆ ◆ ◆

336.

*I believe I should have spent more time
with Mother before she died.*

◆ ◆ ◆

337.

*I believe honor and honesty are
essential in business.*

◆ ◆ ◆

338.

I believe money from inheritance should be considered a bonus instead of money you are depending upon.

◆ ◆ ◆

339.

I believe in wearing comfortable shoes when traveling.

◆ ◆ ◆

340.

I believe in going to the dentist twice a year.

◆ ◆ ◆

341.

I believe the government should balance the budget every year unless, of course, there is a world war.

◆ ◆ ◆

342.

I believe the day will come sooner than later when my daughters will be able to beat me in croquet **and** *tennis. (I am praying that it will be at least ten years before they beat me in golf.)*

◆ ◆ ◆

343.

I believe experience is a great teacher.

◆ ◆ ◆

344.

I believe in doing my best to get along with difficult people.

◆ ◆ ◆

345.

I believe I will get a hole in one before I die.

◆ ◆ ◆

346.

I believe Barbara Walters is a gossip and a voyeur, not a journalist.

◆ ◆ ◆

347.

I believe in teaching my children proper English.

◆ ◆ ◆

348.

I believe Harry Connick, Jr., is a very good actor who just happens to be a more gifted musician.

◆ ◆ ◆

349.

I believe in being loyal to your hometown.

◆ ◆ ◆

350.

I believe couples should hold hands for at least three minutes every day.

◆ ◆ ◆

351.

I believe George Stephanopoulos told more about President Clinton et al. in his book, **All Too Human,** *than he should have. (After all, Clinton is the one who gave him a pretty good job.)*

◆ ◆ ◆

352.

I believe Val Kilmer would be a much better actor if he took his acting more seriously than he takes himself.

◆ ◆ ◆

353.

I believe farmers are the heart and soul of our country.

◆ ◆ ◆

354.

I believe the Beatles' **White Album**
is their best.

◆ ◆ ◆

355.

*I believe John Feinstein is the
world's best golf writer.*

◆ ◆ ◆

356.

*I believe I should pay my wife a
sincere compliment every day.*

◆ ◆ ◆

357.

I believe in walking out of bad movies.

◆ ◆ ◆

358.

I believe my wife is an incredible mother.

◆ ◆ ◆

359.

*I believe big things happen after you
do the little things.*

◆ ◆ ◆

360.

I believe Al Gore is honest but boring.

◆ ◆ ◆

361.

I believe everyone should read The
Adventures of Huckleberry Finn.

◆ ◆ ◆

362.

*I believe you can be compassionate
(care about your fellow man)
and conservative (fiscally responsible).*

◆ ◆ ◆

363.

*I believe I am very lucky to have
been born in a democracy.*

◆ ◆ ◆

364.

*I believe thinking **about** the box is
often more important than thinking
outside the box.*

◆ ◆ ◆

365.

I believe in wearing over-the-calf socks
when wearing a suit and tie.

◆ ◆ ◆

366.

I believe the good big man
will beat the good small man—
if their hearts are of equal size.

◆ ◆ ◆

367.

I believe a great wit and a knack for math
are inherited talents.

◆ ◆ ◆

368.

*I believe the Ryder Cup players
should be paid and the players on the
winning side should get substantially more
money than the losers. (In fact, I would like
to see the winners take all.)*

❖ ❖ ❖

369.

*I believe my desire "to have it all"
is unrealistic.*

❖ ❖ ❖

370.

I believe doctors should at least look interested when patients come to see them.

371.

I believe weekend naps are a great escape.

◆ ◆ ◆

372.

I believe in getting to work on time.

◆ ◆ ◆

373.

*I believe parents are the most
important teachers in a child's life.*

◆ ◆ ◆

374.

*I believe little girls are sugar and spice
and all things nice.*

◆ ◆ ◆

375.

*I believe in trying and, therefore,
in making mistakes.*

◆ ◆ ◆

376.

I believe in recycling.

◆ ◆ ◆

377.

*I believe one man or woman can
make a difference.*

◆ ◆ ◆

378.

I believe luck, chance, and fate can have as much influence on our lives as preparation, organization, and dedication.

◆ ◆ ◆

379.

I believe a life lived on a plateau is truly boring.

◆ ◆ ◆

380.

I believe being loyal is a virtue.

◆ ◆ ◆

381.

*I believe in wearing long-sleeved shirts
with a jacket and tie.*

◆ ◆ ◆

382.

*I believe I could live five lifetimes
and never develop the talents to be a
competent mechanic or carpenter.*

◆ ◆ ◆

383.

*I believe in the big bang theory of how the
universe was created.*

◆ ◆ ◆

384.

I believe Minute Maid orange juice tastes better than Tropicana.

◆ ◆ ◆

385.

I believe in drinking skim milk.

◆ ◆ ◆

386.

I believe birth order does influence our personalities.

◆ ◆ ◆

387.

I believe all work and no play makes me a dull boy.

◆ ◆ ◆

388.

I believe Saturday morning with my family, the newspaper, and a breakfast of pancakes and sausage is as good as it gets.

◆ ◆ ◆

389.

I believe connections can get you an interview and sometimes even get you a job, but after that performance will determine your future.

◆ ◆ ◆

390.

I believe in saving money today so there will be a financial safety net for my children later.

◆ ◆ ◆

391.

I believe a slow wallet can ruin a friendship.

◆ ◆ ◆

392.

*I believe older men with trophy wives have
two things: lots of money and big egos.*

◆ ◆ ◆

393.

*I believe that the bastards win more often
than they should.*

◆ ◆ ◆

394.

I believe in following my heart, unless, of course, it doesn't make financial sense.

◆ ◆ ◆

395.

I believe in giving a person the benefit of the doubt until he proves he doesn't deserve it.

◆ ◆ ◆

396.

I believe there is too much on-field, on-court, on-ice trash talking in professional sports.

◆ ◆ ◆

397.

*I believe boredom and laziness go
hand in hand.*

◆ ◆ ◆

398.

*I believe capitalism is imperfect,
but any alternative is more imperfect.*

◆ ◆ ◆

399.

*I believe we all need to be nicer to each
other. (I think this is one belief we should
all agree upon.)*

◆ ◆ ◆

400.

*I believe the definition of a friend is
someone you call when you have really
great news or really sad news.*

◆ ◆ ◆

401.

*I believe the pace of life in the Northeast
Corridor of the United States is too fast—
too many people in a small space.*

◆ ◆ ◆

402.

*I believe the innocence of childhood reminds
parents that life can be fun, magical,
and amazing.*

◆ ◆ ◆

403.

I believe coffee makes each day possible.

◆ ◆ ◆

404.

*I believe it is better to apologize than
to compromise.*

◆ ◆ ◆

405.

*I believe curious people change
their minds frequently.*

◆ ◆ ◆

406.

*I believe life controls people, not the
other way around.*

◆ ◆ ◆

407.

I believe my daughters should stop growing.

◆ ◆ ◆

408.

I believe **God only knows** *a lot of things.*

◆ ◆ ◆

409.

I believe the addict (alcohol or drugs)
must be allowed to hit bottom before
there is any hope of recovery.

◆ ◆ ◆

410.

I believe in keeping body and soul together for as long as possible (preferably for about eighty years).

◆ ◆ ◆

411.

I believe fishing would be fun if you didn't have to get to the water, get the bait ready, and then clean the ones you are going to eat.

◆ ◆ ◆

412.

*I believe I can get my golf handicap
down to 8 (9 is the lowest it has ever been),
and if I do I will lose lots of bets to
my friends.*

◆ ◆ ◆

413.

*I believe in dressing appropriately
for the occasion.*

◆ ◆ ◆

414.

*I believe in setting realistic goals
and then setting new ones if necessary.*

◆ ◆ ◆

415.

*I believe the death of my mother
will always hurt.*

◆ ◆ ◆

416.

*I believe you should take your children
to bookstores and libraries as often
as possible.*

◆ ◆ ◆

417.

I believe everybody loves to
receive a compliment.

418.

I believe a discreet gratuity to the maître d' can often get you a table sooner or the table you want.

❖ ❖ ❖

419.

I believe Aquavit is the best restaurant in New York City.

❖ ❖ ❖

420.

I believe in miracles.

❖ ❖ ❖

421.

I believe I am the same person I was
twenty-five years ago; however,
the mirror tells a different story.

◆ ◆ ◆

422.

I believe the president of the
United States should be our moral
as well as our political leader.

◆ ◆ ◆

423.

I believe that I will learn to make better
use of my time—next year.

◆ ◆ ◆

424.

*I believe good character
is more important than tons of talent.*

◆ ◆ ◆

425.

*I believe in the Golden Rule:
Always treat others as you would
like them to treat you.*

◆ ◆ ◆

426.

*I believe good table manners
are important.*

◆ ◆ ◆

427.

I believe in checking the gas gauge before I drive off. (I learned this lesson the hard way—twice.)

◆ ◆ ◆

428.

I believe snobs are insecure and a bit afraid of life.

◆ ◆ ◆

429.

I believe it is difficult to take, but well-intentioned criticism can help you to improve.

◆ ◆ ◆

430.

I believe anybody who is cruel to animals should be put in jail.

◆ ◆ ◆

431.

I believe my wife would go backpacking with me if indoor bathrooms were available.

◆ ◆ ◆

432.

I believe most directions to toys, TVs, radios, VCRs, furniture, cars, et cetera confuse the consumer rather than help the consumer.

◆ ◆ ◆

433.

I believe men over thirty-five should not grow ponytails, especially to compensate for a lack of hair on top.

◆ ◆ ◆

434.

I believe my wife now knows all of my hot buttons, and she uses them to maintain control of the household.

◆ ◆ ◆

435.

I believe one tattoo is one too many.

◆ ◆ ◆

436.

I believe far too many questionable words are allowed to air on TV and radio these days, especially during prime time.

◆ ◆ ◆

437.

I believe I should start a diary.

◆ ◆ ◆

438.

I believe life should get easier and less complicated as you get older. Unfortunately, that hasn't been my experience.

◆ ◆ ◆

439.

I believe the world's leaders, including the Pope, need to deal with the issue of overpopulation.

◆ ◆ ◆

440.

I believe the University of Notre Dame is a fine college with an unbelievably lucrative TV contract for its football team.

◆ ◆ ◆

441.

I believe I will be a better dancer in my next life.

◆ ◆ ◆

442.

I believe my mother's death finally made me realize that her advice to me was right more often than not.

◆ ◆ ◆

443.

I believe bureaucrats should learn that rules and regulations must be used in conjunction with intelligence and common sense.

◆ ◆ ◆

444.

I believe it is impossible to fool God.

◆ ◆ ◆

445.

I believe Dr. Laura does her best to remind parents that their children come first.

◆ ◆ ◆

446.

I believe committees ruin or kill more good ideas than they create.

◆ ◆ ◆

447.

I believe the NBA needs to raise the basket by six inches and increase the length and width of the court. (The players today have outgrown the game James Naismith invented over a hundred years ago.)

◆ ◆ ◆

448.

*I believe success begins with the
following daily routine:
(1) Wake up. (2) Get out of bed.
(3) Shower. (4) Get dressed.
(5) Go to work.*

◆ ◆ ◆

449.

*I believe the Academy Awards should
add a "best comedy" category.*

◆ ◆ ◆

450.

*I believe business is an ongoing series of
adjustments and improvements.*

◆ ◆ ◆

451.

I believe Big Bird understands his audience better than any other entertainer.

◆ ◆ ◆

452.

I believe gossip columnists are pretend journalists who far too often care more about pleasing their readers than about telling the truth.

◆ ◆ ◆

453.

I believe the 1964–65 Boston Celtics were the best basketball team ever. (Bill Russell was the league's MVP that year.)

◆ ◆ ◆

454.

I believe that I will go through life without ever seeing a UFO.

◆ ◆ ◆

455.

I believe a man's or woman's word should be worth something.

◆ ◆ ◆

456.

I believe that a good business deal allows all of the partners to make a profit.

◆ ◆ ◆

457.

*I believe everyone needs to have priorities.
(My priorities are family, friends, God,
work, and golf.)*

◆ ◆ ◆

458.

*I believe in measuring twice and
cutting once. (I also believe in hiring
a good carpenter if the project is the
least bit complicated.)*

◆ ◆ ◆

459.

*I believe anger is a legitimate emotion that
needs to be dealt with, not ignored.*

◆ ◆ ◆

460.

I believe gentleness is a quality that works at home and at work.

◆ ◆ ◆

461.

I believe that painful life lessons are rarely forgotten.

◆ ◆ ◆

462.

I believe a little shared information to the field can result in a lot of new sales.

◆ ◆ ◆

463.

I believe Richard Nixon was a crook.

◆ ◆ ◆

464.

I believe women's evening gowns should be elegant and graceful, not showy and busy.

◆ ◆ ◆

465.

I believe minivans are the most practical form of transportation for traveling salespeople.

◆ ◆ ◆

466.

I believe Major League Baseball needs a profit-sharing plan that gives small and medium markets a chance to compete against the big markets. If it doesn't get one, then in a few years there will be six to eight haves and all the rest will be have-nots.

◆ ◆ ◆

467.

I believe cats and dogs should be neutered. (Yes, breeders are exempted.)

◆ ◆ ◆

468.

I believe Jeff Gordon is exciting and Dale Earnhardt is ho-hum.

◆ ◆ ◆

469.

*I believe the greatest artists also have been
the bravest in terms of being true
to their vision.*

◆ ◆ ◆

470.

*I believe Pete Rose is exactly where he
should be—not in the Hall of Fame.*

◆ ◆ ◆

471.

*I believe each day can be my
best day ever—or my worst day ever.*

◆ ◆ ◆

472.

*I believe I have the right to be jealous
of youthful exuberance.*

◆ ◆ ◆

473.

*I believe toupees draw attention to
the fact that you are bald.*

◆ ◆ ◆

474.

*I believe in putting lots of ice in
my cocktails and soft drinks.*

◆ ◆ ◆

475.

I believe I inherited my parents' lack
of talents. (My dad can draw and can't sing
at all, while my mother could carry a tune
but couldn't draw a stick figure.
I can't do either.)

◆ ◆ ◆

476.

I believe a blade razor gives a
closer shave than an electric razor.

◆ ◆ ◆

477.

I believe the remote control ranks as
one of the top ten inventions of all time.

◆ ◆ ◆

478.

I believe Morton's of Chicago is the best restaurant in Chicago.

◆ ◆ ◆

479.

I believe it's not over till it's over.

◆ ◆ ◆

480.

I believe every man wants a Humvee.

◆ ◆ ◆

481.

I believe FAO Schwarz is the best toy store in the world.

◆ ◆ ◆

482.

I believe memories are treasures
that are worth far more than gold.

483.

I believe Tennessee Williams was absolutely right when he said: "The only thing worse than a liar is a liar that's also a hypocrite!"

◆ ◆ ◆

484.

I believe idealists are well-intentioned people who have no common sense.

◆ ◆ ◆

485.

I believe I understand my actions about 70 percent of the time. (The rest of the time I am either totally surprised or disappointed.)

◆ ◆ ◆

486.

I believe I would be rich today if I had the guts to follow my gut instinct.

◆ ◆ ◆

487.

I believe there is a heaven and a hell.

◆ ◆ ◆

488.

I believe I would go crazy if I ever again had to go on a cruise that lasted more than two nights. (How many hours can you spend eating?)

◆ ◆ ◆

489.

*I believe in maximizing my potential.
(Of course, there's the possibility
I already have.)*

◆ ◆ ◆

490.

*I believe bad hair days lead to
costly mistakes at work.*

◆ ◆ ◆

491.

*I believe sports trivia
is* **essential** *information.*

◆ ◆ ◆

492.

I believe Baby Ruth is the best candy bar in the world.

◆ ◆ ◆

493.

I believe in using family names when naming children.

◆ ◆ ◆

494.

I believe a high IQ is just one of many talents God has made available to us.

◆ ◆ ◆

495.

I believe astrology is fun but has no relationship to reality.

◆ ◆ ◆

496.

I believe I can lose a little weight, but it will never be quite enough.

◆ ◆ ◆

497.

I believe Jerry Springer should be ashamed of himself.

◆ ◆ ◆

498.

I believe **Seinfeld** *is the best*
TV comedy ever.

◆ ◆ ◆

499.

I believe M*A*S*H *is the*
second best ever.

◆ ◆ ◆

500.

I believe all men would give up their jobs
to become CIA agents.

◆ ◆ ◆

501.

*I believe existentialism and Christianity
are inherently compatible.*

◆ ◆ ◆

502.

*I believe Barry Goldwater was
one politician who said what he believed.*

◆ ◆ ◆

503.

*I believe the facts that support my
convictions and beliefs. (This is something
we should all guard against.)*

◆ ◆ ◆

504.

*I believe that I am beginning
to think like my father.*

◆ ◆ ◆

505.

*I believe that I am starting
to look like my father.*

◆ ◆ ◆

506.

*I believe my father is very wise
and very handsome.*

◆ ◆ ◆

507.

*I believe—really believe—that giving
is more fun than receiving.*

◆ ◆ ◆

508.

*I believe the feminist movement has had
a positive influence on this country.*

◆ ◆ ◆

509.

*I believe my daughters should have
every opportunity to succeed in
their chosen professions.*

◆ ◆ ◆

510.

I believe Robert Frost put life into proper perspective when he wrote "Forgive, O Lord, my little jokes on Thee And I'll forgive Thy great big one on me."

◆ ◆ ◆

511.

I believe there is a difference between working hard to be successful and being greedy.

◆ ◆ ◆

512.

I believe that the word "hate" should be banned from the English language unless it is used in the same sentence with either "lima beans" or "brussels sprouts."

❖ ❖ ❖

513.

I believe white supremacists have constitutional rights. (I guess that's the price we have to pay for living in a democracy.)

❖ ❖ ❖

514.

I believe you get what you pay for when you stay at a Ritz-Carlton hotel.

❖ ❖ ❖

515.

*I believe casino gambling can be fun
for an hour or two once or twice a year.*

◆ ◆ ◆

516.

I believe man will get to Mars in my lifetime.

◆ ◆ ◆

517.

*I believe we must quickly deal with
the ethical and legal issues of cloning.*

◆ ◆ ◆

518.

*I believe in world peace. (That is probably
more of a wish than a belief.)*

◆ ◆ ◆

519.

I believe I should become an optimist.

◆ ◆ ◆

520.

I believe in signing organ donor cards.

◆ ◆ ◆

521.

I believe you can give good friends unsolicited advice.

◆ ◆ ◆

522.

I believe in picking up after myself. (My wife believes I can still improve in this area.)

◆ ◆ ◆

523.

I believe broken homes too often make life very confusing for children.

◆ ◆ ◆

524.

I believe cheating is wrong.

◆ ◆ ◆

525.

I believe it's okay for men to cry, except during a movie.

◆ ◆ ◆

526.

I believe I would have enjoyed the movie **Titanic** *more if I hadn't known the ending.*

◆ ◆ ◆

527.

I believe I will enjoy James Taylor's songs for the rest of my life.

◆ ◆ ◆

528.

I believe **People** *magazine is fun to read.*

◆ ◆ ◆

529.

I believe Mark McGwire and Sammy Sosa have reminded us that baseball is a game, not just a business.

◆ ◆ ◆

530.

I believe Nietzsche is a bore.

◆ ◆ ◆

531.

I believe Silver Oak is the best California Cabernet.

◆ ◆ ◆

532.

I believe the egg
came before the chicken.

533.

I believe the accordion is the instrument of choice in hell.

◆ ◆ ◆

534.

I believe this quotation is right on the mark: "Everybody should believe in something; I believe I'll have another drink." (Numerous people are given credit for this statement.)

◆ ◆ ◆

535.

I believe capital punishment is justified in cases where a child has been killed or abused.

◆ ◆ ◆

536.

I believe professional wrestling should be
rated for content and language
just like the movies.

◆ ◆ ◆

537.

I believe the Gettysburg Address is
an American treasure.

◆ ◆ ◆

538.

I believe Little League coaches should
concentrate on teaching fundamentals and
good sportsmanship and not
on winning.

◆ ◆ ◆

539.

*I believe Don Imus is really funny
and interesting.*

◆ ◆ ◆

540.

*I believe Howard Stern is sophomoric
and tedious.*

◆ ◆ ◆

541.

*I believe Tiger Woods will become the
second best golfer in history. Jack Nicklaus
will always be number 1.*

◆ ◆ ◆

542.

I believe anyone who has the ability to remember a joke and then retell it well is amazingly talented.

◆ ◆ ◆

543.

I believe **Sports Illustrated** *is the best magazine—not the best sports magazine—in the world. (It has great writing and wonderful photographs.)*

◆ ◆ ◆

544.

I believe **Vanity Fair** *is the second best.*

◆ ◆ ◆

545.

I believe I need to read or reread some of the great books—Heart of Darkness, For Whom the Bell Tolls, Women in Love, The Razor's Edge, 1984, Catch-22—*instead of murder mysteries and spy novels.*

◆ ◆ ◆

546.

I believe anyone who enjoys a good mystery will love Chinaman's Chance *by Ross Thomas. The book features two great characters, Artie Wu and Quincy Durant.*

◆ ◆ ◆

547.

*I believe there may come a time
when I will need to accept the
responsibility of taking care of my father.
(It will be my pleasure.)*

◆ ◆ ◆

548.

*I believe I always will be protective
of my daughters.*

◆ ◆ ◆

549.

I believe nice guys **can** *finish first.*

◆ ◆ ◆

550.

I believe in using a dictionary
if I don't **know** *how to spell a word.*

◆ ◆ ◆

551.

I believe blind dates are a risk
worth taking.

◆ ◆ ◆

552.

I believe the secret of life is having
a kind and generous heart.

◆ ◆ ◆

553.

I believe Vietnam was a painful life lesson.

◆ ◆ ◆

554.

I believe in teaching my children to be nice, honest, and a bit cynical.

◆ ◆ ◆

555.

I believe great pitching beats great hitting.

◆ ◆ ◆

556.

I believe a headstone is the perfect place to make a little life statement. Mine is going to read: He was a critic of the Warren Report.

◆ ◆ ◆

557.

I believe I could make some good investments if I could read tomorrow's paper today.

◆ ◆ ◆

558.

I believe Pat Oliphant is the best political cartoonist in America.

◆ ◆ ◆

559.

I believe the actor Tony Randall was way too old to become a first-time father. (He had his first child at age seventy-seven in 1997.)

◆ ◆ ◆

560.

*I believe Colin Powell would be
a very good president.*

◆ ◆ ◆

561.

*I believe in neighborhood schools
as long as the teachers
and facilities are first-rate.*

◆ ◆ ◆

562.

*I believe my mother was right when she
told me: "The most sophisticated people
are the ones who can get along with
anybody in virtually any situation."*

◆ ◆ ◆

563.

*I believe the **Today** show is the best morning show on TV.*

◆ ◆ ◆

564.

I believe the Old Course in St. Andrews is the best golf course I have ever played.

◆ ◆ ◆

565.

I believe my golfing life will be complete if I ever get to play Royal Dornoch in Scotland.

◆ ◆ ◆

566.

*I believe my wife is
the most beautiful woman in the world.*

◆ ◆ ◆

567.

*I believe Gwyneth Paltrow is
the second most beautiful.*

◆ ◆ ◆

568.

*I believe there is a good chance
that I will go through life **without**
my fifteen minutes of fame.*

◆ ◆ ◆

569.

*I believe my younger daughter, Ruth,
will always be able to depend upon
my older daughter, Cate.*

◆ ◆ ◆

570.

*I believe the whole world needs to know
that a Kansas City strip steak is the same
cut as the New York strip and the name
KC strip came first.*

◆ ◆ ◆

571.

I believe all adults should have up-to-date wills.

◆ ◆ ◆

572.

*I believe there should be work requirements
for welfare recipients—in most cases.*

◆ ◆ ◆

573.

*I believe in mixing cereals. (My favorite
combination is Wheat Chex and Cheerios.)*

◆ ◆ ◆

574.

*I believe Phil Knight, the founder
and CEO of Nike, knows marketing.*

◆ ◆ ◆

575.

I believe margaritas are the perfect summer vacation drink.

❖ ❖ ❖

576.

I believe the political adviser Dick Morris is a small man.

❖ ❖ ❖

577.

I believe a round of golf should be played in four hours, fifteen minutes or less.

❖ ❖ ❖

578.

I believe Dennis Rodman should be more concerned about setting a good example for his daughter than about working on his rebel image.

◆ ◆ ◆

579.

I believe Tom Hanks, John Travolta, Jack Nicholson, and Harrison Ford are the four best actors in Hollywood today.

◆ ◆ ◆

580.

I believe a sense of humor
is *the* essential ingredient
to living.

581.

*I believe Lyle Lovett's hairstyle
works for him.*

◆ ◆ ◆

582.

*I believe that when you hear or read about
Teddy Kennedy, the first thing that pops into
your mind is Chappaquiddick.*

◆ ◆ ◆

583.

*I believe the home underdog
in football is usually a good bet.*

◆ ◆ ◆

584.

I believe Adam and Eve could have lived happy and productive lives without ever knowing about the existence of good **and** *evil.*

◆ ◆ ◆

585.

I believe Benjamin Franklin was indeed America's first Renaissance man. (Did you realize he was a printer, writer, scientist, and statesman?)

◆ ◆ ◆

586.

I believe Jell-O is a food group unto itself and should never be served as dessert.

◆ ◆ ◆

587.

I believe I should do sit-ups and push-ups every day. (Well, how about every other day?)

◆ ◆ ◆

588.

I believe shag carpeting disappeared for a reason.

◆ ◆ ◆

589.

I believe synchronized swimming should be the exclusive domain of women.

◆ ◆ ◆

590.

I believe education should be everybody's top social priority.

◆ ◆ ◆

591.

I believe members of Augusta National (that's the club where the Masters is played) are lucky ducks.

◆ ◆ ◆

592.

I believe men who get pedicures have too much money **and** *too much time on their hands.*

◆ ◆ ◆

593.

I believe a gin and tonic requires a wedge of lime, not a mere slice.

◆ ◆ ◆

594.

I believe Jim Brown (running back for the Cleveland Browns from 1957 to 1965) is the greatest offensive player in NFL history.

◆ ◆ ◆

595.

I believe Jack Ham (linebacker for the Pittsburgh Steelers from 1971 to 1982) is the greatest defensive player in NFL history.

◆ ◆ ◆

596.

I believe the perfect ham sandwich uses rye bread and has Swiss cheese, lettuce, tomato, mayonnaise, and hot mustard.

◆ ◆ ◆

597.

I believe life is complicated and, therefore, can't be simplified.

◆ ◆ ◆

598.

I believe self-deception is a lot easier than self-improvement.

◆ ◆ ◆

599.

*I believe lava lamps must have a place,
but, for the life of me, I can't figure out
where it is.*

◆ ◆ ◆

600.

*I believe the Temptations were the best
Motown group ever. (Isn't "My Girl" great?)*

◆ ◆ ◆

601.

*I believe regular exercise clears the mind as
well as helps the body.*

◆ ◆ ◆

602.

*I believe in getting signed contracts
from contractors who work on my house.*

◆ ◆ ◆

603.

*I believe the New Age movement is
a trend that is getting old.*

◆ ◆ ◆

604.

*I believe February is the most depressing
month of the year—by far!*

◆ ◆ ◆

605.

*I believe I am the most normal person
in my family.*

◆ ◆ ◆

606.

*I believe we need to be more vigilant
than ever in stopping the proliferation
of nuclear weapons.*

◆ ◆ ◆

607.

*I believe it is almost impossible to give your
children too much praise when they have
been especially good or particularly nice.*

◆ ◆ ◆

608.

*I believe children say the
darnedest things.*

◆ ◆ ◆

609.

*I believe teenagers do the
damnedest things.*

◆ ◆ ◆

610.

I believe French fries need ketchup.

◆ ◆ ◆

611.

I believe hamburgers do too.

◆ ◆ ◆

612.

I believe Bill Maher is genuinely funny and **Politically Incorrect** *is entertaining.*

◆ ◆ ◆

613.

I believe I will always remember my SAT scores, but I wish I couldn't.

◆ ◆ ◆

614.

I believe the clause "because I am the parent" should put an end to an argument with my children, but it rarely does.

◆ ◆ ◆

615.

I believe the federal income tax laws and forms should be dramatically simplified.

◆ ◆ ◆

616.

I believe presidential elections should be decided by popular vote instead of by the electoral college.

◆ ◆ ◆

617.

I believe that 90 percent of fitness equipment bought from an infomercial goes unused within six months of being purchased.

◆ ◆ ◆

618.

*I believe four earrings per person
are about enough.*

◆ ◆ ◆

619.

*I believe Pope John Paul II has done
as much for the cause of democracy
as any man in history.*

◆ ◆ ◆

620.

*I believe that if you loan a friend money,
you should think of it as a gift.
(If you actually need the money,
then don't make the loan.)*

◆ ◆ ◆

621.

*I believe men look silly in fur coats—
real or faux.*

◆ ◆ ◆

622.

*I believe in get-rich-quick schemes—
as long as they are quite aboveboard.*

◆ ◆ ◆

623.

*I believe Bill Gates and Microsoft
are guilty of being* **much** *better than
their competition.*

◆ ◆ ◆

624.

I believe raw carrots are better than cooked carrots.

◆ ◆ ◆

625.

I believe in leaving spiders alone— unless my wife tells me otherwise.

◆ ◆ ◆

626.

I believe God and man will work together to save our planet.

◆ ◆ ◆

627.

I believe the parents of the bride should pay for the wedding if they are financially able to do so.

◆ ◆ ◆

628.

I believe in dressing in layers when I am going to be outside on a cold day.

◆ ◆ ◆

629.

I believe that you have to at least **listen** *to advice from people older than you.*

◆ ◆ ◆

630.

I believe a leather couch is a luxury that is worth having. (It will last two lifetimes.)

◆ ◆ ◆

631.

I believe the ladybug is the nicest and prettiest bug.

◆ ◆ ◆

632.

I believe children and adults need to have heroes.

◆ ◆ ◆

633.

*I believe that I will always remember
the day my father bought an "official" home
plate and painted three smooth rocks white
to create a real infield in our backyard.*

◆ ◆ ◆

634.

*I believe my daughters will take care of me
when I am old and rickety. (That's not to
say I will move in with them.)*

◆ ◆ ◆

635.

*I believe my life would take a serious turn
for the worse if I ever forgot my wife's
birthday or our anniversary.*

◆ ◆ ◆

636.

I believe it would be better to be an anteater than an ant.

❖ ❖ ❖

637.

I believe Planters should put more cashews and fewer peanuts in their cans of mixed nuts.

❖ ❖ ❖

638.

I believe avoiding trouble is better than dealing with trouble. (Why can't children understand that?)

❖ ❖ ❖

639.

*I believe arrogant people have
self-confidence but lack a sense of humor.*

◆ ◆ ◆

640.

*I believe my biggest mistakes in business
come when I make assumptions.*

◆ ◆ ◆

641.

*I believe atheists will be pleasantly or
unpleasantly surprised when they die.*

◆ ◆ ◆

642.

*I believe very few people can really tell the
difference between a $750 and a $5,000
sound system.*

◆ ◆ ◆

643.

*I believe highly accomplished artists,
musicians, and athletes are born
and then work very hard.*

◆ ◆ ◆

644.

*I believe women are more sensitive
than men.*

◆ ◆ ◆

645.

*I believe being a high school student
is a full-time job and students shouldn't
work unless their families absolutely
need the money.*

◆ ◆ ◆

646.

*I believe Patty Hearst did willingly help
the Symbionese Liberation Army. (I also
believe Jimmy Carter was right in
pardoning her after twenty-two months
in jail.)*

◆ ◆ ◆

647.

*I believe paying a mortgage is better
than paying rent in almost every situation.*

◆ ◆ ◆

648.

*I believe I am too vague too often when it
comes to dealing with my future.*

◆ ◆ ◆

649.

*I believe in this definition of God:
God is the greatest thing that which
you can conceive.*

◆ ◆ ◆

650.

I believe one of life's great joys
is holding a baby.

651.

I believe China will be a fully working democracy within fifteen years.

◆ ◆ ◆

652.

I believe the debate about genetically manipulating human beings will still be raging in a hundred years. (In my next life, I want to be 6'1" and 190 pounds instead of 5'8¾" and 155 pounds.)

◆ ◆ ◆

653.

I believe shorter is better when it comes to speeches, presentations, and toasts.

◆ ◆ ◆

654.

I believe husbands and wives should do everything possible to protect each other when life becomes difficult or cruel.

◆ ◆ ◆

655.

I believe Maya Angelou was exactly right when she wrote in her autobiography **Singin' and Swingin' and Gettin' Merry Like Christmas,** *"If you have only one smile in you, give it to the people you love. Don't be surly at home, then go out in the street and start grinning 'Good Morning' at total strangers."*

◆ ◆ ◆

656.

I believe soap operas would be better if each episode had a conclusion.

◆ ◆ ◆

657.

I believe the 1927 New York Yankees were the best Major League Baseball team ever. (New York was 110–44 in the regular season and swept Pittsburgh in the World Series.)

◆ ◆ ◆

658.

I believe the Tribune Tower in Chicago is the most beautiful tall building in North America. (It was built in 1925 and is thirty-six stories high.)

◆ ◆ ◆

659.

I believe Jesse Ventura is entitled to his opinion on organized religion, but he was stupid to express it publicly.

◆ ◆ ◆

660.

I believe "Pistol" Pete Maravich of Louisiana State was the most entertaining college basketball player ever.

◆ ◆ ◆

661.

I believe what my grandmother taught me:
Walk on the right side of the sidewalk.

◆ ◆ ◆

662.

I believe in supporting teachers when it
comes to discipline issues.

◆ ◆ ◆

663.

I believe H. Ross Perot is a very talented
businessman and a woeful politician whose
ego won't allow him to listen to his
constituents.

◆ ◆ ◆

664.

I believe a dying person has the right to die and doctors should be allowed to help.

◆ ◆ ◆

665.

I believe the University of Nebraska's 1971 football team, which finished 13–0, is the greatest college team ever.

◆ ◆ ◆

666.

I believe Heinz ketchup is the best ketchup.

◆ ◆ ◆

667.

I believe Lew Alcindor (that was Kareem Abdul-Jabbar's name in college) of UCLA was the most valuable player in college basketball history.

◆ ◆ ◆

668.

I believe Tom Brokaw is the best news anchor on TV.

◆ ◆ ◆

669.

I believe the United States has the right to limit immigration, but we should never close our borders to refugees who need help.

◆ ◆ ◆

670.

I believe the top ten LPs since 1963 (I was in sixth grade in 1963–64) are

1. **Highway 61 Revisited**
by Bob Dylan (1965)
2. **Parsley, Sage, Rosemary and Thyme**
by Simon and Garfunkel (1966)
3. **The Doors**
by the Doors (1967)
4. **Temptations' Greatest Hits**
by the Temptations (1967)
5. **Are You Experienced?**
by the Jimi Hendrix Experience (1967)

6. **The Beatles** *(The White Album)*
by the Beatles (1968)
7. **Beggar's Banquet**
by the Rolling Stones (1968)
8. **Sweet Baby James**
by James Taylor (1970)
9. **Rumours**
by Fleetwood Mac (1977)
10. **Unplugged**
by Eric Clapton (1992)

671.

I believe the beaches of the Florida panhandle are the prettiest in North America. (The sand is white and the water blue.)

◆ ◆ ◆

672.

I believe every home should have the following: a dictionary, a Roget's Thesaurus, Bartlett's Familiar Quotations, The World Almanac, *the* Bible, The American Red Cross First Aid and Safety Handbook, *the* Zagat Survey America's Top Restaurants, *and a* Rand McNally Road Atlas.

◆ ◆ ◆

673.

I believe it is essential
to remain curious.

674.

I believe that fellow Minnesotans Garrison Keillor and Jesse Ventura will eventually find some common ground and become friends. (Their search for common ground may take a little time and effort.)

◆ ◆ ◆

675.

I believe in taking my children to the zoo once a year because it is fun and educational.

◆ ◆ ◆

676.

I believe in paying my credit card bills immediately.

◆ ◆ ◆

677.

I believe Billy Crystal is **very** *funny.*

◆ ◆ ◆

678.

I believe Sonic makes the best fast-food milk shakes and malts by far.

◆ ◆ ◆

679.

*I believe the primatologist Dian Fossey
(1932–85) was a true citizen of the world.*

◆ ◆ ◆

680.

*I believe women can look great in all black,
but men rarely do.*

◆ ◆ ◆

681.

*I believe tractor pulls are massively boring
and waste a lot of gasoline.*

◆ ◆ ◆

682.

*I believe showers are more refreshing
than baths.*

◆ ◆ ◆

683.

*I believe John F. Kennedy, Jr., would have
decided to enter politics, and I believe he
would have been elected president.
(He had all the charm in the world
and very little baggage.)*

◆ ◆ ◆

684.

I believe my father and every other man and woman who served our country in the military during World War II are heroes.

◆ ◆ ◆

685.

I believe the world is a better place because Mohandas Gandhi lived in it.

◆ ◆ ◆

686.

I believe **Pulp Fiction** *can be seen time and time again.*

◆ ◆ ◆

687.

I believe it would be very difficult to be Madonna's daughter.

◆ ◆ ◆

688.

I believe intelligence is ultimately measured by accomplishment.

◆ ◆ ◆

689.

I believe a firm mattress and two soft pillows make for a good night's sleep.

◆ ◆ ◆

690.

I believe my brother is totally trustworthy.

◆ ◆ ◆

691.

*I believe in keeping my tires inflated at
the proper air pressure.*

◆ ◆ ◆

692.

*I believe the disco craze of the 1970s
was a cruel joke on my generation and
was created and perpetuated by the
military-industrial complex.*

◆ ◆ ◆

693.

I believe "Silent Night" is the most beautiful Christmas carol.

◆ ◆ ◆

694.

I believe McDonald's should introduce Happy Meals for adults.
(Adults like free stuff too.)

◆ ◆ ◆

695.

I believe Oprah has succeeded on TV for so long because she still likes her job.

◆ ◆ ◆

696.

I believe we have company
in the universe, and someday
"one of them" will pay us
an official visit.

697.

I believe these are the twenty-three most memorable songs of the last forty years (in chronological order):

1. "Louie Louie"
by the Kingsmen (1963)
2. "She Loves You"
by the Beatles (1963)
3. "You've Lost That Lovin' Feelin'"
by the Righteous Brothers (1964)
4. "My Girl"
by the Temptations (1965)

5. "(I Can't Get No) Satisfaction"
by the Rolling Stones (1965)
6. "The Sounds of Silence"
by Simon and Garfunkel (1965)
7. "Purple Haze"
by Jimi Hendrix (1967)
8. "Brown-Eyed Girl"
by Van Morrison (1967)
9. "Soul Man"
by Sam and Dave (1967)
10. "With a Little Help from My Friends"
by the Beatles (1967)

11. *"I Heard It Through the Grapevine"*
by Marvin Gaye (1968)
12. *"Come Together"*
by the Beatles (1969)
13. *"Fire and Rain"*
by James Taylor (1970)
14. *"Brown Sugar"*
by the Rolling Stones (1971)
15. *"You're So Vain"*
by Carly Simon (1972)
16. *"Cat's in the Cradle"*
by Harry Chapin (1974)

17. "50 Ways to Leave Your Lover"
by Paul Simon (1975)
18. "Dreams"
by Fleetwood Mac (1977)
19. "Beat It"
by Michael Jackson (1983)
20. "What's Love Got to Do with It?"
by Tina Turner (1984)
21. "The Power of Love"
by Huey Lewis and the News (1985)
22. "Harlem Shuffle"
by the Rolling Stones (1986)
23. "Tears in Heaven"
by Eric Clapton (1992)

◆ ◆ ◆

698.

*I believe John Lennon was exactly right
when he said this about love:
"We've got this gift of love, but love is like a
precious plant. You can't just
accept it and leave it in the cupboard
or just think it's going to get on by itself.
You've got to keep watering it.
You've got to really look after it
and nurture it."
(Lennon said this on television in 1969.)*

❖ ❖ ❖

699.

I believe stereotypes are right enough often enough to be dangerous.

◆ ◆ ◆

700.

*I believe Harry Truman was the last president who **loved** being honest and open with the public.*

◆ ◆ ◆

701.

I believe prayer works.

◆ ◆ ◆

702.

*I believe people do judge you by the
company you keep, and that's okay.*

◆ ◆ ◆

703.

I believe old friends know you best.

◆ ◆ ◆

704.

*I believe even good plans need
adjustments and refinements.*

◆ ◆ ◆

705.

*I believe I need to spend more
time thinking.*

◆ ◆ ◆

706.

*I believe all words, sentences, and
paragraphs form images in my mind.*

◆ ◆ ◆

707.

I believe one hour of
creative thinking is often
more productive than ten hours
of analyzing minutia.

708.

I believe the United States is making progress in race relations, but it will be another four or five generations before race won't be much of an issue.

◆ ◆ ◆

709.

I believe Sunday nights are a bit depressing even though I don't have any homework.

◆ ◆ ◆

710.

I believe Bon Ami is the best household cleaner on the market.

◆ ◆ ◆

711.

I believe it's your turn to write down some beliefs and then share them with your family and friends.

◆ ◆ ◆

◆ ◆ ◆

Dear Reader,

Are you willing to share your beliefs with others? I would love to know what some of your beliefs are and then put some of them into a book. Take a few minutes to think about what you believe and then send them to me either via mail or e-mail. If you send any of your beliefs to me, I will assume that I have your permission to use your name and the content of your correspondence in any future books or calendars. It would be great if you would include something about yourself—name, age, sex, occupation, where you live, etc.

My address is: Allan Stark
                Stark Books/Andrews McMeel Publishing
                4520 Main Street
                Kansas City, MO 64111

My e-mail address is: IBelieve@AMUniversal.com

I am looking forward to hearing from you.